UNSCARRED!

WALKING THROUGH THE ASHES OF THE PAST

BY:

EVERLENA OLIVER

Unscarred!

Walking Through The Ashes of The Past

By

Everlena Oliver

Copyright @ 2018, All Rights Reserved
Printed in The United States of America

Published By:

ABM Publications
A division of Andrew Bills Ministries Inc.
PO Box 6811, Orange, CA 92863

ISBN: 978-1-931820-91-2

All scripture quotations, unless otherwise indicated are taken from the King James Version of the Bible, Public Domain. Those marked AMP are from the Amplified Bible, copyright @ 1987, The Updated Edition, by the Zondervan Corporation and the Lockman Foundation, and is used by permission. All rights reserved.

DEDICATIONS

To my parents, Jinnie and Eddie Coleman, who raised me in a strong Christian home.

To my husband and six children who stayed by me as I went to college and later to work.

To my proof reader, Lenora Mitchell who was not afraid to tell me what she thought I should expand on or change.

And last but not least, my mentors, typists, and publishers, Pastor Ann Marie Bills and her husband, Apostle Andrew Bills of The Holy Spirit Broadcasting Network, who always encouraged me to write my story.

CONTENTS

	Introduction – Walking Through The Ashes of The Past	vii
1	Walking By Faith – From Texas To California	9
2	How Big Is Your Giant? - "Mr. Cool."	15
3	Reaching The Top According To God's Plan - Finishing High School	21
4	Marriage – The Early Years	23
5	Walking Through The Fire - Years of Infidelity	25
6	Reaching The Top According To God's Plan - The First Years of Marriage	31
7	Finding The Way - Going Back To Church	33
8	Rising Above Your Circumstances - Going To College and Having Two Careers	37

9	Rising Out of The Ashes - Is There Life After Retirement?	39
10	The Fruits of A Prayerful Life - Seeing God's Blessings In My Family	43
11	My Road To A Career	45
12	Fear Is Just A Word, Not The End	49
	CHRISTIAN BIO	51
	CAREER BIO	53

INTRODUCTION

Walking Through The Ashes Of The Past

Have you ever felt like a loser or even less because you made some wrong choices or decisions in your past? What is the definition of insanity? Doing the same thing repeatedly and expecting different results.

Author Everlena Oliver: wrote "Unscarred: Walking Through The Ashes of The Past" for all and everyone who need and wants more faith, courage and most of all, God's good grace. I am here to tell you that you are not alone, and God will never leave your side. I am living proof that through Christ we can do all things which strengthen me. (Philippians 4:13).

You need to throw your ashes in a peaceful place and let it go. Ashes can weigh a lot on your shoulders even though it doesn't look heavy. I am going to share some amazing testimonies about my life and how I made it through the fire, storm, wind and lightning and God was there by my side the whole time. I realize that having faith and a positive mind and energy is key to beating any negativity in your life. No matter how bad it can be, every day above ground is a blessing. I dare you to read this book and better your life. It only takes one day at a time to make a change for the better. Because you bought this book you are already making a change. Once you start to read it, you will not put it down. It is not about just reading it, it is about learning and applying it to your life. Take control and be the Author of your fate. You must block out all the negativity and haters.

Focus on what matters the most = God and you and nothing else. So, I leave you with this: Be encouraged and reach high for your purpose in life. Above all always pray for revelations and your purpose in life. Pray and ask God what your gift is. Because your gift will make room for you.

CHAPTER ONE

WALKING BY FAITH FROM TEXAS TO CALIFORNIA

Early on the morning of January 3, 1946, I made my arrival. I was born to a fifteen year old unwed mother. She was at home with a midwife because the nearest hospital was miles away. It was a small Texas town named Avinger. The man I called dad for 18 years was with her. He was around 18.

When I was 18, my mother told me the man I had known as dad all my life, was not my biological dad. All I knew about my biological father was his name. I never met him. There were no pictures of him and he never tried to see me as far as I know. At first I was sad but then realized I had a good dad that cared for me and was there for me all the time.

Back then in this small town, my mother was ostracized from the other girls her age. She was tainted. People talked about her behind her back. Her mother had put her out and her dad had been dead about two years by this time. Alone and afraid, she was offered a job at a local cleaners where she met the man that would later marry her.

His family was upset and didn't want him to marry her. After the courthouse wedding, his dad gave him land across the road from the main house. He built a small house and there we lived about 3 years. Then he got an offer to go to Orange County, California with my mother's uncle named Walter Lewis, the brother of her mother. It would be him, his wife and his four children and another family called the Stewarts and their children. My mother and I stayed behind because there was no room in the old truck they were traveling in.

After about 4 days, they arrived in El Toro, California. They found a compound of four houses down from a rail road station which had a small country store.

The next smallest town was called Laguna Beach, where they were able to find jobs. "Dad" found a construction job with a company called Miller's Construction located in the Laguna Canyon.

After a while, he saved enough money to send for my mother and me. I was 3 years old when we boarded a train headed to California. I had a great time eating and sleeping on the train. I had no sense of time but was told later it took us about 4 ½ days. We arrived at a large train station in a city named Los Angeles and began our new life in California.

We lived in El Toro about six months. My dad then rented a two bedroom house in the canyon from his boss, next to the McClure's, a family of two boys. From there we moved to the town of Laguna on 3rd Street in an apartment across from the local lumber yard, behind a large Presbyterian church and across from the Laguna fire station and police department. The address was 2nd and Forest Avenue. The other relatives found housing one street over on Ocean Avenue.

Later my mother registered me to attend school at Marie Thurston Elementary which later became the intermediate school when El Moro Elementary was built and opened during my 2nd grade year. It was a beautiful school overlooking the ocean. We were able to see the whales when they migrated down our coast.

Our principal was Mr. Allan. I became friends with his daughter, Leslie, because she was in my class. The pastor was Mr. Young of the Presbyterian Church in front of our house. His daughter, Connie, was also in my class. I started attending the church and remained a member until I graduated from high school.

My other classmates, Nancy White, Belinda Blacketer, Lyn Williams, and Claire and Vickie Pell, where friends from 1st grade through 12th grade.

I guess that period of my life was blessed. I grew up being the only black child in a predominant Caucasian school and town. I was the only child in my family until I was 9. My mother then had my brother and soon after a sister and by the time I was in junior high, another sister.

After a few years, my family bought a house on Woodland Drive in the Canyon. There was another black family living across the street from our house. They ended up having nine children, so I had plenty of playmates. There was a divorced mother of 2 up the street. They were also black. There was a boy and girl. The girl was a year younger than me but she became my best friend.

I remember evenings of playing kickball outside of our house until the porch lights came on. We also went back and forth to each other's houses. Then a tragedy struck my friend. Her mother died when we were in elementary and she and her brother had to go live with their father in San Francisco and I never saw her again. This was also my first experience with death. I was scared to view her body, but I eventually walked by the casket. I was surprised that she just looked like she was asleep.

EVERLENA OLIVER

CHAPTER TWO

HOW BIG IS YOUR GIANT?
"MR. COOL"

My peaceful life changed when I was 13. The family next door had an uncle visit for that summer. He was 16 and even though I was not into boys yet, whenever I was around him I felt funny.

About 2 months after he came, his brother and wife asked my parents if I could go to the drive in with them in Santa Ana. Actually I guess it was located in Costa Mesa. The brother and his wife had two small children, so the 4 of us sat in the back seat because of the children, we were sitting pretty close.

During the middle of the first movie, he let his arm fall around my shoulder, where it remained during the first movie. Then, at intermission, we walked to the snack bar making small talk. He said he had a girlfriend back home in Bakersfield, but she had gone on vacation someplace (my red flag should have gone up because he was getting pretty familiar with me). During the second movie he snuck a kiss. It was the first time I had ever been kissed by a boy. I didn't know what to think. Later that week, I was down at my girlfriend's house and the phone rang. When she answered it, she made a funny face because it was him. Of course I had told her about the kiss at the movies. She handed the phone to me and I pretended to be her.

He thinking I was her, starting flirting with her who was actually me. After about 5 minutes, I told him he was speaking with me. He tried to play it off that he knew it was me. Red flag number two. He was a player. But I didn't have the sense enough to realize his game. Later that summer, our neighbor's mother, dad, and sisters moved to Laguna. I became friends with the daughter that was my age. They lived down town on Ocean Avenue.

My next red flag was I found out Mr. Cool had taken her out and kissed her. She didn't know he had also kissed me. I of course was hurt, then angry, but he smoothed it out by saying he really didn't like her and that I was the one he really liked. As the summer came to an end, he went back to Bakersfield and I didn't see him again until I was 16, when I went up to Bakersfield to spend 2 weeks with his brother and sister-in-law, who were friends with my parents. I still did not have a boyfriend and actually had not thought of having one.

Soon I met a boy that was a friend of my mother's friend. He was a high school student one year ahead of me. He played varsity football and was planning to go to college after he graduated in June. We became friends, however, later that week, Mr. Cool came back into my life. He came over to visit his brother and I.

Of course, he was staying in Bakersfield. He soon asked his brother if he could take me to the show with his sister and her husband and children. The answer was yes as I would be chaperoned by their sister and her husband. We walked to the cars and I headed to his sister's car and he took my hand and led me to his car. My stomach had an uneasy feeling because I was to ride with his sister and family. He said it would be okay because we would be at the same movie.

As we pulled into the theater, I saw his sister and family went toward the front and we went to the back. Again I felt uneasy and told him I wanted to park next to them. He said it would be okay if we parked in the back. The first movie was fine and at intermission we walked over to his sister's car and said, "Hi!", and asked if they wanted something from the snack bar. They said no so we went on our way.

Ten minutes into the next movie he made his move. He pulled me over to himself and started to get aggressive at which time I tried to push him away. He kept trying to kiss me and I said no. At this point, he became angry and said he was taking me home. I said okay and he did. When he let me out of his car, I could hear his tires squeal as he took off.

I didn't see the other boy again but my mother's friend said he had asked about me from time to time. Afterward I went back to Laguna. As for Mr. Cool, I didn't hear from him again until that fall when he moved to Garden Grove to live with a brother and his family. It turned out he had gotten into some trouble and his parents wanted him to change environments. He dropped out of school, moved in with his brother and got a job.

I didn't know he was back until one night I was going to a football game in Orange and I rode with his brother and his brother's daughter, who was 2 years in back of me in school. Her older brother was 1 year behind me in school and it was his game we were going to attend. I was told we were going to stop in Garden Grove to pick up her uncle. I was surprised to find out it was Mr. Cool.

We talked and enjoyed the game. Later, we dropped him off and went home. A few weeks later, he moved to Laguna with the brother that lived across the street, the one with 9 children. By that time, I was 16 and we started to see each other. He said he and his girlfriend were no longer seeing each other. My parents, especially my dad, did not want me to date him. They wanted me to concentrate on school and plans to go to college. They were not pleased that he had dropped out of school.

The next red flag was when I invited him to be my date to the senior prom. I had get special approval from my principal. Mr. Cool was 18 and did not attend school. My mother took me to a boutique in Corona Del Mar to get a dress and to the beauty shop to get my hair and nails done. When the big day came, I waited until 11p.m. and he never showed up or called.

I was devastated. I was thinking something had happened to him. It turned out he was stranded at this brother's house that lived in Garden Gove. He didn't think to call me and let me know he couldn't make it. Needless to say, my dad said this was more of a reason I didn't need to see him anymore. He was like a magnet to me. He was the bad boy, like

James Dean or the guys in West Side Story. He was a challenge and I felt special that he had chosen me over his other girlfriends. Did opposites really attract?

My dad had been an excellent example as to how a man treats a lady. He always treated my mom with respect. I never saw them argue or cuss at each other. He treated her like the queen she was. He made sure she didn't have to work and yet he bought her a new car every 3 years and always made sure she could go to the beauty shop to get her hair and nails done.

When my dad saw me crying the day Mr. Cool didn't show up for my senior prom, he said you are crying now but if you marry him, you will spend many days crying. I thought at that time, my dad was just talking. I truly believed I would love him so much that he would change his life style just to make me happy.

CHAPTER THREE

REACHING THE TOP ACCORDING TO GOD'S PLAN - FINISHING HIGH SCHOOL

Meanwhile, I went on to do my high school activities with my friends. We were like minded and all planned to attend college after high school. We were in the same clubs at school and played the same sports. None of us really had a steady boyfriend.

One friend liked a young marine stationed at Camp Pendleton, so we would go with her to visit him on base at their movies. My friend Vicky and I had crushes on our varsity basketball players. They never acknowledged us. Years after I graduated from high school, I read what the boy I had liked had written in my year book. He said he would have asked me out if I hadn't been so stuck up.

He mistook my shyness for being stuck up. I often wondered how my life would have been had we hooked up. He went on to graduate from Arizona State and on to play professional football for a few years, and then became a businessman.

I met my future husband again when he moved to Garden Grove to live with his older brother. We started to date during my junior year. One of my biggest disappointments was for senior prom. I got all dressed up in my new dress, had my hair and nails done and he never showed up. No phone call or message. The next time I saw him he was so casual like it was no big deal that he hadn't shown up. That should have been a red flag warning for me but I forgave him and went on with the relationship.

He actually showed up for my graduation and for the grad night party.

CHAPTER FOUR

MARRIAGE – THE EARLY YEARS

Meanwhile, Mr. Cool came in and out of my life. When I was a senior he asked me to marry him and gave me a beautiful engagement ring. I graduated and was married in August of that same year. We had planned to marry in July but found out we needed birth certificates. His from Bakersfield, where he was born, and mine from Texas, where I was born. I was upset because I felt getting mine would take weeks. Actually it didn't. We could still be married in July.

The second time we were going to go down to Santa Ana to the old court house. We were going to be there at 10 a.m. I wanted to wait for Mr. Cool to come. By 4 p.m. I knew it wouldn't be that day. Later that evening he came over and said his brother had left him on a job they had been dong and he was stranded with no ride and the wedding band was in his brother's car. I didn't take those two incidents as a warning and proceeded to marry him on August 3rd, 1964 in Santa Ana.

We got married with my mother and a friend being our witnesses. We had our own apartment but no car. Soon we lost our apartment because my husband was working with his brothers and didn't have a steady paycheck. We then had to move in with his brother and his family and five children and two other brothers and one of the brother's girlfriends. The girlfriend and I slept on the couch. My husband and his brother slept on chairs. To make matters worse, I was now pregnant and going to Santa Ana College.

My mother finally said I could come back home but I would have to sleep on the couch because my cousin from Texas was now living with her and my two sisters and brother in a 3 bedroom house. My husband now had a stable job at Saddleback Inn in Santa Ana but made only minimum wage and no benefits. Soon my cousin felt sorry for me and let me have my old room back.

The next year in March, our son was born. He was beautiful and was my motivation to give him a good life by finishing college so I could get a good job. When he was about 6 weeks old, we moved back to Laguna to live with my dad. My dad helped my husband to get a construction job and to join the local 652 union. We were able to buy a car and get our own apartment in Santa Ana. This was the time I began to walk in the fire.

CHAPTER FIVE

WALKING THROUGH THE FIRE - YEARS OF INFIDELITY

We had been married less than a year and had been living in Laguna. We were invited to a party by his brother. My mother-in-law kept our baby and we went to the party. After about an hour, I asked my sister-in-law if she had seen my husband. She said, "No." So thinking he had gone back to the car for something, I went outside and started to walk down the street where the car was parked. Then I saw him.

He was kissing some girl we had met at the party. They looked like one body, they were so close. He looked up and saw me and asked me what I was doing there. I lunged at her and proceeded to hit her. I was jealous, angry and sad at the same time. She ran back up the hill to the party and I didn't see her again. I knew I was wrong and I shouldn't have hit her.

Emotions do strange things to you. We left the party and I cried all the way home. Our sacred vows had been broken. We made up and then moved back to Santa Ana to our apartment.

It wasn't long before I busted him with another girl that had been friends with me at our new apartment. She was married and had a 3 year old daughter. They lived 2 apartments down from us. We were both very young. She and my husband had been sneaking around about three months before I saw them go into our little laundry room and turn the lights out. I was crushed again.

The next day, my mother happened to come over and I asked her to take me and my son up to Los Angeles to stay with my aunt. She called my aunt and made sure it was okay. My aunt welcomed us to her home. It was during the riots in Los Angeles and Compton. It was very frightening. We had a curfew and had to be off the streets by 6 p.m. We could hear gun shots and had to sleep on the floor away from windows.

I knew I had to get my son to safety so I asked my cousin to take us back home, which he did. When we arrived at my apartment, he made me stay in the car to make sure I wouldn't be walking into a situation. He came back and said no one was home. He helped me and the baby get settled before he left.

About two hours later, my husband walked in. His face was swollen with a cut above his eye. He said he had given a party the night before and had gotten into the car and was driving in the fog and that he had been drinking. He hit 3 parked cars on First Street and had totaled our car. Again, we had no transportation.

We made up again. The next day his girlfriend stood outside my door saying all kinds of nasty things to me as she was moving out. It seems her husband had found out about their affair and decided enough was enough and had left her. I didn't see her again for about 20 years. Ironically, I ended up serving her at a church dinner in my church. She didn't know who I was but I heard her ask her sister who I was.

My heart dropped to my feet and I asked my Christian friend what I should do. She said, "Ask her which part of the chicken she wanted." I was serving the chicken. It was one of the hardest things I had to do. I said, "Lord, what is this about? Why do I have to humble myself to serve her?" I wondered what my husband would do when he saw her.

Life went on and we were blessed to buy a house. We were also blessed to have 3 children by then. A boy and two girls. My husband continued to have his flings. By then I had a government job at FHA which later became HUD (Housing & Urban Development). I was about to buy a car for myself. I had put the kids in nursery school down the street from my job. My husband was still getting his jobs through the union; however, when he wasn't working, he would hang out with his drinking friends and when he had my car, he wouldn't pick me and the kids up. I had to walk to the nursery school, pick them up, and then walk over to the liquor store where he and his friends would be sitting in my car drinking. I would put them all out and go home.

Another tragic event that occurred during my Laguna days was the day after my graduation from high school; my mother woke me up and said to pack all my things that I wanted, because we were moving. I didn't know what to think. My parents had never argued in front of us and never displayed anything but love for each other. Later I learned that my mother's friends had been influencing her to leave my dad. Funny though, once she left, the friend that was talking the most, ended up dating my dad. Lesson learned, don't let your friends into your marriage. Talk to the Lord. I guess my mother had planned to leave for a while because she already had a 3 bedroom house she had rented in Santa Ana. She had been moving her personal items a little at a time. The plan that day was to leave while dad was at work, which we did. She had waited until I graduated to make her move. I believe that is one reason I married two months later. We moved out to our own apartment. As I said before, that only lasted about four months before we couldn't pay our rent and ended up living from house to house.

CHAPTER SIX

REACHING THE TOP ACCORDING TO GOD'S PLAN - THE FIRST YEARS OF MARRIAGE

During the first year of marriage, I started thinking more and more about the Lord. I had not been in church since my mom moved us to Santa Ana. I finally decided I needed to find me a church home. My hair dresser invited me to attend her church.

It was a small Methodist church on Bristol and Second Street. I attended there for about a year by myself. Then my husband started cheating on me and I went to the pastor for counseling and he thought I wanted money from the church and he told me the church could not help me financially, to which I told him I didn't want the church to give me money. I needed guidance as to what to do. He advised me to get a divorce and set me up with his son-in-law who was a new attorney.

I never felt comfortable getting a divorce but I listened to the pastor and other family members and ended up filing for a divorce. All I really wanted to do was to establish legal child support for my 4 children, which was set up through D.A.'s office.

We went to court where the judge awarded me child support and said we should get another court date in a few months for the final filing of the divorce. I prayed again and the Lord showed me scripture that stated, "What God has joined together no one can break apart." It is a covenant with the Lord, man and his wife. My soul was uneasy. I didn't want to break God's covenant. I also did not want to raise my children in a broken home.

Since I was also pregnant with our fourth child, I definitely did not want to bring another child into the world without his dad being in his life. After our son was born, we went back together. The baby was four months old. He never apologized for what he had done.

CHAPTER SEVEN

FINDING THE WAY - GOING BACK TO CHURCH

I eventually dropped the divorce and we went back together and tried to mend our marriage. Meanwhile, I went back to college and earned an AA in business management. I changed churches and went to a new church up the street from our new house, a Baptist Church. My husband would only attend with us (the kids and me) on holidays such as Father's Day & Christmas and maybe Easter. I got my children involved in the children's activities, such as choir and Sunday evening youth training and I became an usher.

I ended up quitting my job at HUD and went back to college getting a degree as a L.V.N. and one year later an R.N. Then I was blessed to go on to Cal State Fullerton to earn a degree as a B.S.N. When I graduated, I had six young children. I then started my career as an oncology nurse at UCI Medical working the swing shift. This allowed me to be home to get my children ready for school and be home when they came home from school. For the most part, my husband had a separate life. He still lived at home but his routine was to come home from work, take a shower and hit the streets. On Fridays, he would get paid. I wouldn't see him again until Monday. He would come home, get ready for work and leave. Needless to say, the check had been spent during the weekend.

We lived like that for a few years until he became sick and was hospitalized for nearly a year. His doctors didn't know what was causing him to have high temperatures at night and difficulty breathing. Finally, a doctor was able to diagnose that he had asbestos in the lining of one of his lungs. He ended up in surgery where he lost 1/3 of his lung. It took him a year to get his strength and weight back. He had gone down from 175 to around 90 lbs. He quit smoking and drinking for one year but on the day he was released from medical care, he went back to smoking and drinking and being unfaithful.

I came home one day, from staying at the hospital with his niece, when her young daughter was in surgery. I knew something was strange when I walked in the door. When I went into the bedroom, I saw empty drawers open and the closet (his) was empty. My worst fear, he had moved out and left me and the kids. No note, no phone call, no anything to explain to me why. I soon found out he had a girlfriend and had moved in with her. She was a single mom with a small son. I was blindsided.

It seemed his brother, sisters, and nephew knew but I didn't. This time I was pregnant as I said before with our 4th child. That relationship only lasted a few months, but he went on to move in with another girlfriend and was with the second one when I went into labor. His new girlfriend called the hospital and told me she had told him he needed to be at the hospital with me. I was so hurt; I hung up and just cried. He later came to visit me after I gave birth to our son.

We eventually went back together and I went on to have two more children. I gained another degree and certificate in teaching.

I'm telling my story to help all the young women who think life is over when they make wrong choices. Your mistakes should not define your future. The common thread through all I went through was the Lord was always with me and helping me. The early trials helped me to become who I have become today.

CHAPTER EIGHT

RISING ABOVE YOUR CIRCUMSTANCES - GOING TO COLLEGE AND HAVING TWO CAREERS

The Lord let me have two careers. One as a Special Educator in a local high school for 16 years. I have learned to lean and depend on the Lord in all that I do.

I was also blessed to have a career as a R.N. I received a bachelor's degree in nursing. I went on to work for eleven years as a registered nurse at UCI Medical and St. Joseph's hospital in Orange. The marriage was still a mess but I had money coming in to help pay the bills and to afford to buy my own car.

The Lord led me to return to college and to pursue a career as a special education teacher. I thought being a teacher would give me more time to be with my children. I was blessed to graduate within a year with a master's degree in education and a minor in special education. I was again blessed to get hired on my second job interview with the Santa Ana Unified School District where I worked as a special education history teacher and co-teach with a regular educator who had special education students that may need help to be successful in a regular class.

Those were the most rewarding years of my career because I could see the positive impact on our students. The Lord gave me discernment on how to work with each student to achieve their success.

Over the years I have been blessed to see some of my prior students and to see how they have turned into productive adults. Some even thanked me for being their teacher and for pushing them to work toward their goals and dreams.

CHAPTER NINE

RISING OUT OF THE ASHES - IS THERE LIFE AFTER RETIREMENT?

When I retired from teaching in 2014, the Lord led me to run for the Santa Ana Unified School Board. I wanted to bring a teacher's insight to the board. After all the teacher knows firsthand what the students and teachers need. Most of the board members are business people. There is not one teacher on the board. I still don't know why I was compelled to run. I didn't win a seat but learned a lot about politics.

Then the Lord put it on my heart to tell my story in this book to help young women to move on from wrong decisions to doing better with their lives.

I have a heart to help young women in all walks of life. I have been doing a jail ministry for 4 years at the IRC in Santa Ana. It's very rewarding to help give hope to young women who think their lives are over because they are incarcerated.

My desire now is to do motivational speaking based on biblical principles.

In 2014 I was diagnosed with end stage renal failure. I immediately went into denial and put off dialysis for a few months. After all I was running for an office and wouldn't have time to have dialysis. However, in September of 2014, I ended up in the hospital and while I was there, surgery was done to put in a fistula and a catheter in my chest to start dialysis. I had the catheter for about 5 months in my chest until the fistula was ready to be used.

Meanwhile, I kept all my campaign appointments, not telling anyone about my pending dialysis. I had to have dialysis 3 hours, three times a week. I refused to let even that define what I could not do. Because I was busy running for office, I didn't have time to have a pity party. I just did what I had to do.

Since I have been on dialysis, I have seen many patients give up and die. The Lord keeps me strong and I truly believe He will heal me someday, because He has work for me to do in his kingdom and He has not brought me this far to leave me.

I give all credit to my strong faith in the Lord. I didn't mention all the trials I went through with my marriage. There were many, many long nights and lonely days.

I almost lost my 5th child. I woke up in a pool of blood on my sheets. My husband was still out. I got into my car and drove myself to Palm Harbor hospital (which is now Garden Grove Hospital). Before I left I called KYMS Christian radio for Calvary Chapel and asked for prayer. On the way to the hospital, I heard my prayer request and the prayer when I was checking into the ER.

I was put in a room and examined. I was told, other than the blood on my under clothes, there was no evidence that I had been hemorrhaging. There was no internal bleeding. This was evidence that the Lord had intervened. I went on to deliver a normal healthy baby boy.

EVERLENA OLIVER

CHAPTER TEN

THE FRUITS OF A PRAYERFUL LIFE - SEEING GOD'S BLESSING IN MY FAMILY

Another miracle that I witnessed was when I had asked the Lord to allow my children to grow up in one house with a mother and dad and He granted me that prayer. My children had a stable home no matter what was going on with my husband and me. I was able to see each one of the six graduate from high school and some to graduate from college.

Most of my children have careers. My oldest is Pastor (Bishop) of his own Church. One is a financial manager for a realtor. One is a marketing manager working on her Ph.D. One son is a Chief Investigator for the State of Hawaii. Now I am being blessed to see some of my grandchildren to be blessed with degrees and good careers.

Yes, I am still married to the same man for 54 years, come August this year. Is he the same? No. Instead of the clubs he spends most of his time at church. He loves the Lord and has been a deacon for 30 years. This was a major miracle that I was able to forgive and forget all the indiscretions that occurred. Was it painful? Yes. God had a purpose for our trials. We ended up being good role models for our children. They have learned never give up and to trust the lord in all that they do.

My advice to young people is to establish a relationship with the Lord. The earlier the better and know your purpose for your life. As the Lord says in Jeremiah 1:5, "He knew you before you were formed in your mother's womb", and He had a plan for your life. In Jeremiah 29:11, found in the New Living Translation bible, He states you have a purpose.

CHAPTER ELEVEN

MY ROAD TO A CAREER

My first job was at age 16 at a pill factory. I packaged and filled doctor's orders for pills. I did this job after school from age 16 to 18.

After I graduated from high school and was married, I got a telegram from the local unemployment office stating they had a job offer for me from the Federal Housing Authority, better known as FHA, and later named HUD, Department of Housing and Urban Development. I worked there for 11 years and decided to quit and go back to college because I was told I was at a standstill for getting a promotion without a degree. So I quit for a year, got an AA in business management and went back for a year.

I was passed over for another promotion and was told they gave it to new girl because she had some college. I told them I had an AA in business management and they told me in HR they didn't know, which was untrue, because I had given them copies of my transcripts from college. I ended up quitting again.

Our finances became weak so I had to try to find another job to help my husband out. I applied to the Register Newspaper as a proof reader and was allowed to take their typing test. I just knew I had that job because I was classified as a clerk typist for HUD for 11 years. Well, I failed the first typing test and I was allowed to take it again the next week because the HR person really liked me and wanted to hire me, but I had to retake and pass the typing test. I went on to fail the typing test. Somehow I had skipped an entire line on the typing test which caused me to fail.

I was so desperate to find a job that I applied and was hired as a bed maker at a convalescent home. After a week making beds my supervisor said she noticed I was really good with the patients and asked me if I wanted to become a certified nurse's aide and make 75¢ more per hour. Of course I said yes. So within 6 weeks I became a CNA. Then the LVN on my team asked me if I had ever considered being a nurse and she told me I would make more money and have benefits. So I called Santa Ana College to get on their waiting list for the next LVN program. They called me back and said some people dropped out and could I come in for the practical hands on test. I said yes. To my surprise, I only had to make a bed with a patient in bed and a regular bed. Bingo! I had that. I had been a bed maker. Then I had to take vital signs on a patient, which I had been doing as a CNA. Then I found out the 2 classes that were required, I was already enrolled in and due to finish before the semester the nursing program started. Was this by accident? No. The Lord had staged it all. I went on to because an RN the next year and a BSN in the next two years.

Then my company was purchased by another company and the Lord had me one step ahead again. A friend had told me about a new program at Fullerton State that would give you a credential to teach and a master's in Education in one year.

They were only accepting 30 students into the program and over 100 had applied. The Lord came through yet again and I was placed in the program and graduated within a year as a Specialist in Special Education and was able to get a job right after graduation at Santa Ana High School as a 11th grad Special Education teacher, where I retired from in 2014 with 16 years. As I look back, I can see how the Lord paved the way for me.

CHAPTER TWELVE

FEAR IS JUST A WORD NOT THE END OF MY STORY - FOUND OUT FEAR DID NOT ENTER INTO MY JOURNEY

My definition of fear is believing in false evidence appearing to be real.

Now I am excited to see where he takes me with this new stage of my life. I know it's going to be more than I could have ever imagine.

I have learned to trust that God is in control of every facet of my life and that his will be done no matter how it looks on the outside.

Why did I write this book?

I wrote this book mainly because I needed to go through a healing process. I thought I had forgiven my husband but I still had deep rooted resentment, pain, and hurt that I had to resolve. The Lord showed me I had to get rid of that root before I could be healed. The more I shared the more I was relieved.

What did I learn?

As I pondered over my past for lessons learned, I found out sometimes we have to go through the storm to get to the peace. Just as the Hebrews took 40 years to get to the Promised Land, instead of 11 days. Some of us, through disobedience, are allowed to go through self-will. (I became the strong, Christian woman I am today.) I now know where I am and who I am! Would I, looking back, go in that same direction? I would like to think I wouldn't but at the same time, I realize I had to go the way I went in order to be free. The key would have been to believe I needed better. I should have respected myself more. Somewhere along the way, I had low self-esteem and believed he was doing me a favor. I also had to learn to love myself.

My advice to any young woman today would be to apply Matthew 6:33 pray and listen for the Lord's voice in every decision. My number one mistake was to make my husband my God. I now know my joy comes from God. No man can fill that void. You have to be secure in who you are made to be.

CHRISTIAN BIO

1ST church was Presbyterian Church of Laguna Beach, CA, under Pastor Turner, on 2nd and Forest, from 1st grade to 12 grade.

Johnson Chapel for 1 year 1965 – 1966, under Reverend Williams.

2nd Baptist 1966 – 1977, Pastor Kassee

Starlight Baptist, Pastor Ford 1978 – 2011

Greater Light Family Church 2011 – present, Pastor / Bishop Gale L Oliver, Jr.

Started in youth choir at 1st church

Johnson Chapel – no office

Starlight – Mission Choir; Assistant Superintendent, Deaconess, Mission President 1 year, Adult Class Sunday School Teacher (20 years), Pastor's Aide 2 years

Greater Light – Finance Office to present, Vacation Bible School Teacher 3 years, Teacher for Experiencing God on Wednesday am & pm class for 6 months

Jail ministry 4 years to present

Baptized at Presbyterian Church at age 13 (sprinkled)

Rededicated at Starlight Baptist because I understood why I was being submerged in water rather than sprinkled

I love the Lord and now I have a personal relationship with Jesus.

CAREER BIO

2014 Retired from Santa Ana Unified School District with 16 years from 1998 to 2014 (Special Education)

1995 – 1996 Hughes Aircraft Company – Company Clinic Nurse – 1st at Fullerton facility then ended at Long Beach facility

1994 – 1994 VA Hospital 7 months

1994 – 1995 UCI Medical – 3 years oncology nurse and medical surgical and St. Joseph's Hospital 7 months

1996 – 1997 California State University Fullerton – Earned Bachelor's Degree in Nursing

1997 – 1998 Earned Master's in Education with minor in Special Education

1998 – 2014 Worked at Santa Ana High School as a Sprcial Education History teacher (U.S. History)

2014 July Ran for Santa Ana Unified School District Board (did not win)

2014 Haven't worked since 2014, June 20th

1967 – 1978 Worked at HUD for 11 years – Clerk Typist & Insurance Clerk

1964 Graduated from Laguna Beach High School

1962 Summer worked at Laguna Reef Motel in South Laguna as a maid

1963 – 1964 Worked at Pinco after school filling orders for doctor's offices

1964 Junior College at Santa Ana College – earned AA in Business Management and Science, and LVN & RN nursing

Earned Bachelors of Science in Nursing and Masters in Education from California State University Fullerton

www.ingramcontent.com/pod-product-compliance
Lightning Source LLC
Chambersburg PA
CBHW061515040426
42450CB00008B/1632